WALLS

The Long History of Human Barriers
and Why We Build Them

WALLS

The Long History of Human Barriers and Why We Build Them

Gregor Craigie

Illustrated by Arden Taylor

ORCA BOOK PUBLISHERS

Published in Canada and the United States in 2024 by Orca Book Publishers.
orcabook.com

Library and Archives Canada Cataloguing in Publication
Title: Walls : the long history of human barriers and why we build them /
Gregor Craigie ; illustrated by Arden Taylor.
Names: Craigie, Gregor, author. | Taylor, Arden, illustrator.
Series: Orca timeline ; 5.
Description: Series statement: Orca timeline ; 5 | Includes bibliographical references and index.
Identifiers: Canadiana (print) 20230200753 | Canadiana (ebook) 20230200761 |
ISBN 9781459833111 (hardcover) | ISBN 9781459834880 (PDF) | ISBN 9781459834897 (EPUB)
Subjects: LCSH: Walls—Social aspects—Juvenile literature. | LCSH: Walls—History—Juvenile literature. | LCSH: Walls—Juvenile literature. | LCSH: Human geography—Juvenile literature.
Classification: LCC TH2201 .C73 2024 | DDC j721/.209—dc23

Library of Congress Control Number: 2023934953

Summary: Part of the nonfiction Orca Timeline series, with photographs and illustrations throughout, this book explores why and how people have built walls all over the world throughout the course of human history.

Orca Book Publishers is committed to reducing the consumption of nonrenewable resources in the production of our books. We make every effort to use materials that support a sustainable future.

Orca Book Publishers gratefully acknowledges the support for its publishing programs provided by the following agencies: the Government of Canada, the Canada Council for the Arts and the Province of British Columbia through the BC Arts Council and the Book Publishing Tax Credit.

Author photo by Rebecca Craigie
Cover and interior artwork by Arden Taylor
Design by Rachel Page
Edited by Kirstie Hudson

Printed and bound in South Korea.

27 26 25 24 • 1 2 3 4

In memory of my dad,
Peter Craigie

Contents

INTRODUCTION

If you walk out the front door of the post office in the village of Beebe Plain, Vermont, and turn left, you'll find a road called Canusa Street about 50 feet (15 meters) away. Standing on the south side of the road and looking north, you're gazing from the United States of America into its next-door neighbor, Canada. All that separates the two countries is a double yellow line painted down the middle of the road. Sure, there's a border crossing beside you, where drivers going to the town of Stanstead, Quebec, check in with border guards. But there's no giant concrete wall standing between the two countries. No chain-link fence. No barbed wire. Just a road with two yellow lines.

A lot of the world's borders are like this. They're either invisible to people standing on the ground or difficult to see. But more sections of America's southern border with Mexico now have walls or fences separating the two sides. And America isn't alone. Around the world, more countries are building border fences and walls, from Bangladesh to Bulgaria and beyond. Human-built barriers can stretch for thousands of miles across some pretty wild terrain. Many of these walls are relatively new. But the desire to build walls that separate us from others is almost as old as humanity itself.

THE OTHER SIDE

They have been built for different reasons—to protect crops and livestock, and to make it easier to collect money from taxpayers, to name two. But most great walls were built to keep the people inside safe and to keep out the people thought to be dangerous. Some of the walls worked, and ones that may be built in the future could make some of the people who built them feel more secure. But what about the people on the *other side*? We should consider them when we look at why people build walls. And we should think about *why* they might want to cross borders—and get past the wall—in the first place. Experts who study the reasons for human migration—people moving from country to country—say the effects of climate change and inequality are both huge factors. While the world keeps building barriers, we can't forget the forces that make people move in the first place.

American and Canadian road signs, side by side, in the Vermont village of Derby Line. While many of the world's borders have walls, there is no such barrier between these two countries. The house behind the road signs is in the United States. The customs inspection building, just past the house, is in Canada.
ERIKA J. MITCHELL/SHUTTERSTOCK.COM

The Great Wall of China
700 BCE–1644

Ukraine's Ancient Walls
200 BCE–700

The United States–Mexico
Border Wall
1909–present

Hungary Border Barrier
2015

One

TO KEEP PEOPLE OUT

In recent years many countries, from Argentina to Uzbekistan, have been busy building new barriers along their borders in an effort to keep other people out. But there's nothing new about this. Countries and kingdoms around the world have been doing this for thousands of years.

THE GREAT WALL TODAY

The Great Wall of China is a *UNESCO World Heritage site* and is considered one of the great architectural structures in human history. It draws many tourists who want to see the wall up close and walk along it. The Mutianyu section of the wall is the longest one open to tourists and has been called a "masterpiece of restoration" because of the work done to restore the wall and 23 watchtowers. The Badaling section of the wall, near Beijing, was rebuilt in the 1950s to attract tourists to China. Some sections have been made accessible to people in wheelchairs. Other sections of the Great Wall are much rougher and steeper and can be dangerous to anyone walking or climbing along them.

THE GREAT WALL OF CHINA

- *BUILT: 700 BCE–1644*
- *LENGTH: 13,171 miles (21,196 kilometers)*
- *HEIGHT: 20 feet (6 meters) on average, and up to 46 feet (14 meters) in some places*
- *MATERIALS: Rammed earth, stones, wood and brick*

The most famous wall in the world is probably the Great Wall of China. Despite its name, the Great Wall is actually a series of fortifications, linked together across ancient China's northern borders, that were built to keep wandering groups of *nomads* out of the kingdom. Some of the earliest portions were built in the seventh century BCE, before the first emperor of China, Qin Shi Huang, built new sections to join the walls.

It was a huge job. General Meng Tian was put in charge of the project. He used a giant army of soldiers to build it, and probably prisoners too. The working conditions were extremely difficult, and thousands of people died during construction. Some of them are buried inside the wall itself. Most sections of wall were replaced by the *Ming dynasty*, which built the most famous sections of wall between 1368 and 1644.

The Great Wall of China stretches through and over hills. The wall's watchtowers are plainly visible. In total, as many as 25,000 watchtowers were built along the Great Wall.
APHOTOSTORY/GETTY IMAGES

Strong Enough to Stop Galloping Armies

The walls were high enough and thick enough to stop nomadic armies on horseback from galloping into the kingdom. The Great Wall also included **barracks** for Chinese soldiers to live in and watchtowers that gave them good views.

As a defensive barrier, the Great Wall of China had mixed results. It kept many invading nomads out. But Genghis Khan and the Mongolian army breached the wall several times, which let them conquer China and defeat the Jin dynasty. The Mongol Empire founded the Yuan dynasty, which ruled China for about a century. After that the Ming dynasty took over and used the wall to keep the country secure. Not only did the Ming extend and strengthen the wall, they split it into a south and north wall—called the Inner and Outer Walls—to better protect the capital, Beijing.

The Great Wall had other jobs. It served as a road for traders on the famous **Silk Road**—between Asia, the Middle East and Europe—for hundreds of years. It allowed Chinese rulers to control what went in and out of the kingdom and collect **taxes** on those goods.

UKRAINE'S ANCIENT WALLS

People in Europe first built walls more than 2,000 years ago. On the fertile plains of what is now Ukraine, farmers built long walls to protect their crops and livestock and to keep traveling invaders out. The walls worked, and their farming communities grew into empires. The first walls were made of soil and piled in long, straight lines across the flat landscape. There are still about 600 miles (1,000 kilometers) of wall in Ukraine, but at one point there may have been five times that. Long ditches were dug and the soil was piled alongside the ditch to form a wall that was double the height. Although it was a simple solution, the barrier was probably enough to stop nomadic horsemen in their tracks. Historians are not sure who built these walls. It may have been the Scythians, the Goths or the early East Slavs. It's possible all three groups built different sections of wall over hundreds of years.

THE UNITED STATES–MEXICO BORDER WALL

- *BUILT: 1909–present • LENGTH OF BORDER: 1,954 miles (3,145 kilometers)*
- *LENGTH OF BARRIER: 771 miles (1,240 kilometers)*
- *US STATES ALONG THE BORDER: 4 • MEXICAN STATES ALONG THE BORDER: 6*

"I will build a great, great wall on our southern border, and I'll have Mexico pay for that wall." That's what Donald Trump told Americans before he became president. Trump accused Mexico of exporting violent crime and illegal drugs and argued that a wall would stop both. Border guards have seized many illegal drugs and arrested many **migrants** along the border, but Mexican officials point out that illegal activities go both ways across the border—thousands of weapons are **smuggled** from the United States into Mexico every year. Roughly two-thirds of the Mexico–United States border still had no physical barrier when Trump's four-year presidency came to an end. The United States built several relatively short sections of barriers along the border, but most of those were

replacements of older barriers. And, no, Mexico did not pay.

The US government has built a variety of barriers along parts of the border over the last few decades, mainly to stop illegal **immigration** and drug smuggling. The US Customs and Border Protection agency operates 50 border crossings, where roads cross the border, and where drivers need to talk to border guards before they can continue. The agency also uses many miles of fencing to try to stop people walking or running across the border. Steel posts called bollards are cemented into the ground and connected by chain-link fencing. Some of those steel-post fences are as high as 30 feet (9 meters) and are sunk 6 feet (1.8 meters) into the ground to stop people from tunneling under. Roads have also been built along the fence to allow border guards to quickly move along its length. In some areas there are lighting, cameras, **surveillance** technology and three layers of fencing. In the judgment of one report, "it's not a wall, but it's not nothing."

Coming Between Families

Certainly the barriers between the United States and Mexico are not nothing for families divided by them. In some cases Mexican mothers cannot join their children in the United States. Brothers, sisters, uncles and aunts may live in Mexico and may not be permitted to move to the United States. There are many possible reasons why the US government won't let them in—some might not have permission to work in the United States, and others may have been caught trying to cross the border without permission in the past—but the border fences and barriers make the separation seem painfully simple. Is this a compassionate response to people in need? Or a cruel divide between people who should be allowed to come together? Like so many questions about barriers, the answer depends on who answers and on what side of the wall they stand.

HUNGARY BORDER BARRIER

- **BUILT: 2015**
- **LENGTH: 325 miles (523 kilometers)**
- **HEIGHT: 13 feet (4 meters)**
- **MATERIALS: Steel fence and concertina wire**

Hungary has also put up fences along its borders. In 2015 more than a million **refugees** and migrants were making their way to Europe, hoping to find a better life.

It was the highest number of displaced people in Europe since World War II. Most of the people were fleeing the Syrian Civil War, but there were also people from Afghanistan, Pakistan, Iraq and other countries. Most of the migrants were trying to get to countries like Britain, Germany and Sweden but found themselves walking through Eastern Europe to get there. The Hungarian government wanted to stop the tide of people crossing its borders, so in the summer of 2015 it built a barrier along its border with Serbia to stop people crossing who did not have permission. A few months later it built a similar barrier along its border with Croatia, made with concertina wire, a sharp razor wire formed in large coils. The barrier has helped Hungary achieve its goal of reducing illegal immigration, which stopped almost completely. But the move came with criticism from the **United Nations**. Former UN secretary-general Ban Ki-moon said, "We should not be building fences or walls, but above all we must look at root causes."

More and More Walls

In recent years millions of people have fled their home countries because of civil war, extremism, oppression and fear. And scientists worry the climate crisis could make things even worse in the future if we don't do more to stop it. Droughts, floods, heat waves, pandemics and other extreme events might become more common and create more competition for food, water and other resources. If we don't all work toward a world where people are free and safe in all countries, the flood of desperate people isn't likely to stop. Nor is the temptation to build more walls to keep people out.

FRIENDSHIP PARK

There is a park on the border, sandwiched between the Mexican city of Tijuana and the American city of San Diego. Friendship Park is at the very western edge of the border, where the steel wall extends into the crashing waves of the Pacific Ocean. There's a stone monument that sits right on top of the border, and for many years there was nothing more than a rope draped along the border itself. But now there are two sturdy border walls there, and the San Diego Border Patrol closes the space between the walls during weekdays. The park is open for limited hours on some weekends, and when it is, people on both sides meet each other through a steel mesh fence. Many people who are living in the United States illegally visit their families there. Others, who live in the United States legally but do not have the proper travel documents, also go there. Some Mexican grandparents meet their American grandchildren through the barrier. Many people say their final farewell to dying family members the same way.

Two

TO KEEP PEOPLE IN

While some walls were built to keep people out, others were erected with the sole purpose of keeping people inside. Those walls acted like giant prisons, trapping the unwilling inside and making it practically impossible to escape. Such walls made possible some of the cruelest events in history.

As two individual continents, Africa and Europe are separated by the Mediterranean Sea. But there are two exceptions, where land claimed by the European Union borders with Africa. Ceuta and Melilla are autonomous cities that are administered by Spain, which is a member of the European Union. Both cities are located on the coast of Morocco and therefore have land borders with the African country. These are the two land borders between European and African countries and both have security fences. In 2005 Spain built double fences to prevent people from crossing the border illegally and to stop smuggling. Each border has two barriers, standing 20 feet (6 meters) high and topped with barbed wire and razor wire, which is much sharper. While the fences have kept many people in Africa, some migrants have been so desperate to make a better life in Europe that they've climbed over the fences and razor wire. Many have been injured in the process, with some sent to the hospital and at least one man reported to have died from his wounds. Some Spanish politicians have pledged to remove the barriers. But as of 2023 the barriers between Africa and European territory still stood.

WARSAW GHETTO WALL

- *BUILT: 1940* - *LENGTH: 11 miles (18 kilometers)*
- *HEIGHT: 13 feet (4 meters) in total, with wire*
- *MATERIALS: Brick topped with barbed wire*

Poland was home to millions of Jews before World War II. The capital, Warsaw, was a major center of Jewish culture, and almost one-third of its population was Jewish. The Nazis, who ruled Germany under Adolf Hitler, hated Jewish people. When they invaded Poland, they ordered Warsaw's Jews to move into an area of the city that would become known as the Warsaw ghetto. The Nazis surrounded the ghetto with barbed wire at first, then built a brick wall topped with wire, which made it 13 feet high (4 meters) in total. Jewish people from surrounding towns were also forced inside, and the population swelled to over 400,000. It was so crowded that there were more than seven people for every room in the ghetto.

Conditions inside the ghetto were horrific. Without enough food or medicine, more than 80,000 people died of starvation or disease in the first two years. After that the Nazis sent thousands of Jewish people away from the ghetto to die in **concentration camps**. Many of the people who were trapped inside the ghetto fought back bravely during an uprising in 1943. But the Warsaw ghetto wall was one of the cruelest barriers ever built. When Warsaw was liberated in 1945, only 11,500 Jewish survivors were still there.

BERLIN WALL

- *BUILT: 1961 · DEMOLISHED: 1989*
- *LENGTH OF CONCRETE WALL: 66 miles (106 kilometers)*
- *HEIGHT: 11.8 feet (3.6 meters)*
- *MATERIALS: Concrete filled with steel and topped with barbed wire*

When Germany lost World War II, the Nazis were defeated, and the country was divided in two. East Germany was **communist** and allied with the Soviet Union. West Germany was allied with Western countries, including the United States, Britain and Canada. Most of the border between East and West Germany ran through the countryside, but it also divided the capital, Berlin, where East Germany built an imposing concrete wall complete with guard towers, trenches and beds of nails. The wall stopped East Germans from visiting West Berlin, where people enjoyed more freedom and typically had more money.

About 100,000 East Germans tried to escape to the other side, and about 5,000 succeeded. More than 100 people died trying. The mayor of West Berlin, Willy Brandt, called the barrier the Wall of Shame. It stood for 28 years until a series of political revolutions in Eastern Europe convinced East German leaders to tear down the Berlin Wall, thereby lifting the Iron Curtain, as many people called the divide between east and west Europe. People on both sides rejoiced at the news. Friends and family members climbed onto the wall, reuniting after many years. Some chipped away at it, claiming small pieces of concrete as souvenirs. The wall was soon torn down, and East and West Germany reunited into one country.

The Western Sahara Wall also has one deadly feature—a long line of land mines that are buried just beneath the surface along the full length of the wall. There are millions in total, in what has been called the longest minefield in the world. Many people who live in Western Sahara have stepped on mines accidentally and either died or lost legs. Most of the victims have already suffered significantly from the fighting and live in refugee camps on both sides of the barrier. In recent years, Sahrawi refugees and international human rights activists have come together to hold an annual demonstration against the wall—called the Thousand Column—where they link arms to create a human chain and demand the demolition of the barrier.

WESTERN SAHARA WALL

- **BUILT:** *1980–1987* • **LENGTH:** *About 1,700 miles (2,700 kilometers)*
- **HEIGHT:** *Up to 10 feet (3 meters)*
- **MATERIALS:** *Sand and stone, lined with land mines*

Western Sahara is a disputed territory in northwest Africa that was a Spanish colony until 1975. When Spain left, neighboring Morocco invaded the sparsely populated desert territory. But the Sahrawi People, who call Western Sahara home, organized into a rebel group called the Polisario Front and fought a **guerrilla war** to force the Moroccans out. While the fighting continued in the 1980s, the Moroccan government built a long sand **berm** to mark the unofficial border between the two sides and keep the Polisario Front rebels inside a thin strip of desert between that long sand berm in the west and the border with Mauritania in the east. It isn't very impressive to look at, and some travelers have even made fun of it. One called it the Not So Great Wall of the Western Sahara because it isn't very tall. Still, the wall is guarded by thousands of Moroccan soldiers and is covered in **radar** masts and other pieces of electronic surveillance equipment.

An Unofficial Border

After years of fighting, a **ceasefire** was signed that effectively gave Morocco control of the coastline and the western two-thirds of the territory, leaving a thin strip of desert to the Polisario Front until the group ended the ceasefire in 2020. For nearly 30 years, the Western Sahara Wall was the unofficial border between the two sides. It's estimated that less than 100,000 people live in this desert—many of them in refugee camps.

A small group of protesters hold Polisario flags and look at the Western Sahara Wall, or berm, some distance in front of them. Built of sand and stone, the berm is the same color as the desert surrounding it and is difficult to see from a distance.

ISRAELI WEST BANK BARRIER

- *BUILT: 2002–present* · *LENGTH: 440 miles (708 kilometers)*
- *HEIGHT: Up to 26 feet (8 meters)*
- *MATERIALS: Concrete, chain-link fence and barbed wire*

In 2002 the government of Israel started building a wall, saying it needed to protect Israeli citizens from attacks by Palestinians in the West Bank, which Israel has occupied since 1967. Palestinians call it a racial-segregation wall that cuts off thousands of people from their friends and families and isolates large areas of fertile farmland. In cities like Jerusalem, it is a high concrete wall. But for most of its length it is a series of fences, ditches and roads for patrol vehicles on both sides. Some of it is built along the Green Line, which marks the original boundary of Israel. But more than three-quarters of the barrier is built inside the West Bank, effectively separating tens of thousands of acres of land and thousands of Palestinians from the rest of the West Bank. That prevents many from getting to work, school or the hospital. When it was first built, Israel's separation wall was described as temporary, and the United Nations has since demanded its removal. But for now the barrier remains.

SAUDI BARRIERS

Saudi Arabia is much larger than Israel and has borders with several countries. In 2014, with a civil war causing chaos in Iraq, Saudi Arabia started digging a ditch barrier and building a multilayered fence with as many as 78 watchtowers. The 560-mile (900-kilometer) barrier also uses monitoring technology, like radar and night-vision cameras. The Saudi Arabian army even sweeps the desert sand between the fence and an outer sand berm so it can check for footprints of people who might be trying to sneak out of Iraq into Saudi Arabia.

Saudi Arabia has built an even more formidable barrier along its southern border with Yemen, where a civil war has been fought for years. The 1,100-mile (1,800-kilometer) barrier also features a long steel pipeline filled with concrete. Saudi Arabia said the 10-foot- (3-meter-)high barrier would stop attacks from armed rebels with Yemen's Houthi movement. Saudi Arabia is a wealthy country, rich in oil, but Yemen is very poor and the war has taken a terrible toll—tens of thousands of civilians have died, and millions face starvation. While many people in Yemen have friends or family in Saudi Arabia, the barrier has made it all but impossible for them to help.

Long Walls of Athens
461–457 BCE

Amorite Wall
2100–2000 BCE

Machu Picchu
c. 1450

The Red Snake (Great Wall of Gorgan)
c. 420–540

Three

TO PROTECT CROPS AND LIVESTOCK

Most walls protect people, but some were built specifically to protect a community's ability to grow food. In some cases, walls have kept farmers and farmland safe from invading armies. In others, walls have held the land in place so that it could grow food for the communities they surrounded.

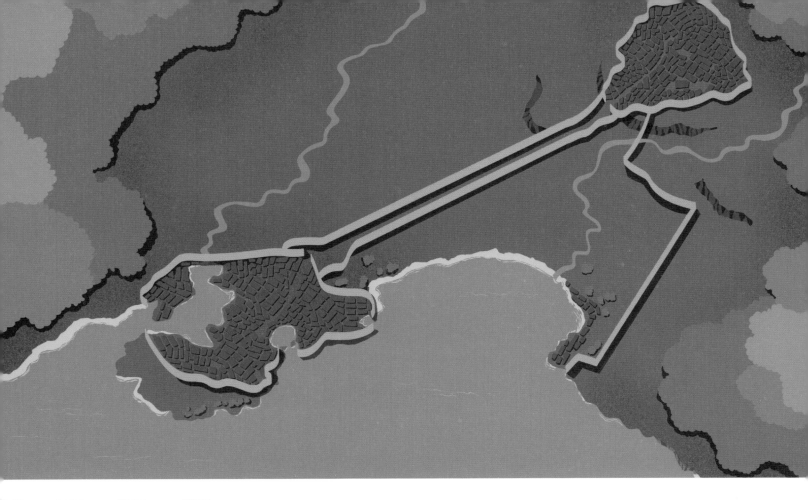

LONG WALLS OF ATHENS

- *BUILT: 461–457 BCE* · *LENGTH: About 4.5 miles (7 kilometers) each*
- *HEIGHT: Up to about 32 feet (10 meters)*
- *MATERIALS: Sun-dried bricks on limestone blocks*

The ancient Greek city of Athens is built in the hills, about five miles (eight kilometers) from the Aegean Sea. In between their impressive city and their powerful navy, the Athenians grew food on fertile farmland. But Athenians realized that farmland was a serious weakness during the Greco-Persian Wars, a series of battles fought between Greek city-states like Athens and the Persian Empire in the fifth century BCE, because it would be relatively easy for the Persian enemy to capture it.

When the Persian king Xerxes the Great attacked Athens in 480 BCE, the Greek general Themistocles proposed two protective walls running from Athens to the coast to form a triangle of land between the city and its ports. The building finally started in 461 BCE, when Athens was at war with another Greek city-state—Sparta. The Spartans had a stronger army than Athens, but the Athenian navy was more powerful. The western wall was built from southwest of Athens to the port of Piraeus. The eastern wall was built to another port, Phaleron, and was slightly shorter than the western wall. The two walls connected the city to the sea and also created a protected area of farmland in between for growing food.

Extra Protection

For added protection, the Athenians later built a second wall running ***parallel*** to the western wall and a series of towers along the length of each. The long walls let Athens survive a ***siege*** from enemy armies, as long as their powerful navy was not defeated at sea. In a later war with the Spartans, many people from the neighboring countryside moved inside the walls, and all Athenians survived on food shipped to the city via Athens' two ports.

So the walls worked when Athens controlled the sea. But when the Athenian fleet was defeated in 405 BCE, the city was cut off from new food supplies, and Athens was forced to surrender to the Spartans, who destroyed the long walls "among scenes of great joy." Athenians rebuilt the walls 10 years later, and they remained standing for another 300 years. When the Roman general Sulla besieged the city, he destroyed the walls once and for all, in 86 BCE.

An old drawing of ships in the Greek port of Piraeus, as well as the two long protective walls that stretch from the port up to the city of Athens in the hills beyond.
JOHN STEEPLE DAVIS/WIKIMEDIA COMMONS/PUBLIC DOMAIN

AMORITE WALL

• BUILT: 2100–2000 BCE • LENGTH: At least 155 miles (250 kilometers)
• WIDTH: 29 feet (8.8 meters) • MATERIAL: Rough bricks

While many ancient walls were built of stone or mud, the Red Snake was made with millions of large red bricks. They were made to a few standard measurements—14.5 inches long (37 centimeters) in western portions of the wall, 15.7 inches long (40 centimeters) in the eastern. The bricks were produced by forming the local *loess* into the proper shapes and then making them hard in thousands of large brick *kilns* that were set up along the wall. In 2005 a team of Iranian and British archaeologists measured a kiln that had been excavated and discovered that its dimensions were nearly identical to another kiln discovered in the 1970s. The kilns were an important clue for archaeologists who wanted to calculate the age of the wall. They dug out samples of the charcoal in the kilns, then used *radiocarbon* and *optical dating* to determine the walls were built during the fifth or sixth century BCE.

Between 2100–2000 BCE the Sumerians of Mesopotamia (modern-day Iraq) built a long wall to protect the city of Ur and the surrounding farmland that gave the city its food. The wall is now known to historians as the Amorite Wall (named after the people it was trying to keep out) or the Wall of Mardu. It wasn't the first wall the Sumerians built. As early as 3500 BCE, Sumerian builders used sun-baked bricks to separate their cities from the fertile farm fields surrounding them. While the farms were crucial to feed the city folk, the walls proved even more crucial when wandering nomads rode in on horseback to attack. During an attack, the people working in the fields would run back toward the city, cross over a small bridge that spanned a moat outside the walls and seek protection in their homes behind the brick walls.

An Advanced Civilization

Behind their wall, the Sumerians had developed a complex civilization that likely included such innovations and inventions as the wheel, chariots, schools, irrigation, monumental architecture, *bureaucracy* and writing. The Sumerians thrived in their cities, thanks in large part to a stable supply of food from the surrounding farms.

While the Amorite Wall was well built, it had a few key problems. The first was that the Sumerians didn't have enough soldiers to guard all of it. The second was that it was not anchored on either end, so an invading army could simply ride around it where it met each river. And that's exactly what the Amorites did. They invaded from the west for many years and weakened the Sumerians. Eventually the Sumerians fell to an invasion from their eastern neighbors, the Elamites.

Bricks were used to build the Amorite Wall in Mesopotamia. The Sumerians also used them to build pyramid-shaped structures, called ziggurats, like this one, which still stands in the ancient city of Kish in modern-day Iraq.
DAVID STANLEY/WIKIMEDIA COMMONS/CC BY 2.0

THE RED SNAKE (GREAT WALL OF GORGAN)

· **BUILT:** c. 420–540 · **LENGTH:** 121 miles (195 kilometers)
· **WIDTH:** 20–33 feet (6–10 meters) · **MATERIAL:** Fired bricks

More than 2,000 years after the Sumerians built their great wall, another civilization built a mighty wall in what is now northern Iran. The Sasanian Persian Empire erected the Great Wall of Gorgan—a long brick structure that stretched from the shores of the Caspian Sea in the west up to the foothills of the Elburz Mountains in the east.

They built the wall to defend the fertile Gorgan plain, where they grew most of their food. Archaeologists think a lot of soldiers—anywhere between 15,000 and 36,000—were stationed along the wall to guard against enemies. The wall was attached to at least 30 forts built along its length. Archaeologists believe the Sasanian engineers were highly skilled, because the smooth, steady angle of the canal next to the wall ensured a constant supply of water to act as a defense against enemies coming from the north. The water in the canal was provided by a series of at least five smaller canals that brought river water from the south. In this semi-arid region that gets little rain, the water could be used both for farming and to help make the millions of bricks that were needed to create the wall.

Lost in the Sands of Time

The wall still stands today, although archaeologists have had to dig much of it out of the ground that covered it, thanks to the wind blowing dust and sand over it for about 1,500 years. The wall is also known as the Red Snake because of the color of the bricks. In fact, the wall has had many names over the years. Persians called it Alexander's Wall because Alexander the Great, the ancient Greek king who conquered the Persian Empire in the fourth century BCE, is thought to have marched through the area.

MACHU PICCHU

Perhaps the best-known walled city in South America is the famed Machu Picchu, which the Incas built sometime around 1450, high in a tropical mountain rainforest more than 7,900 feet (2,400 meters) above sea level, as a royal estate for the Inca emperor Pachacuti. The Incas built a lot of walls in Machu Picchu. Some held up roofs. Others protected the city from enemies. But a lot of the walls were designed to turn steep mountain slopes into farmland.

The rugged mountaintops were not a natural setting for gardens, of course. So the Incas built long walls across the slopes to create flat terraces for growing crops like maize. Once a solid wall was built across a slope, soil would be piled on the uphill side of the wall to create flat ground where crops could be planted in long thin rows. The Incas built many terraces that eventually looked like large, wide green steps leading up to Machu Picchu itself. The *terrace* gardens provided a lot of food, but they were difficult to build and maintain in such a rainy area. When it rained really hard, the extra water would shift some of the stones in the walls, causing landslides.

Living With Llamas

The city itself was divided into upper and lower parts, with most living accommodations in the upper part and the farming below. The latter included many animals, including llamas and alpacas, which are naturally suited to living at high altitudes and grazed on the slopes beneath the walled city. Archaeologists believe people lived in Machu Picchu from 1450 to the 1530s. Between 500 and 1,000 people may have lived there, many of them servants. The walls were built of dry stones, stacked without *mortar*. While some of the stones were likely cut, many chunks of granite may have been produced by earthquakes, which shake the Andes mountains from time to time.

A Historic Legacy

Machu Picchu was abandoned about 100 years later, after the Spanish colonized the area. It is not clear exactly why it was abandoned, but it may have been because so many Inca people died from *smallpox*, a deadly disease that was brought to the Americas by Europeans and may have killed hundreds of thousands of Inca people. Today Machu Picchu is a world-famous historic and tourist site, renowned for its beauty. UNESCO calls it one of the "greatest artistic, architectural and land-use achievements anywhere and the most significant tangible legacy of the Inca civilization."

Llamas continue to live among the ruins of Machu Picchu. They still graze on the steep slopes but can now roam on the flat human-built terraces that were once gardens for the Inca people who built Machu Picchu.
OGPHOTO/GETTY IMAGES

Kuélap
c. 900–1100

Sungbo's Eredo
c. 800–1000

Maginot Line
1928

The Great Wall of India
15th century

Four

TO DEFEND AGAINST THE ENEMY

Maybe the most common reason for building walls is to stop an invading army. From the days of spears and swords through the era of cannon fire—and well into the 20th century—military leaders have put their hopes in strong walls standing up against their enemies.

SUNGBO'S EREDO

- **BUILT:** c. 800–1000
- **LENGTH:** Estimates range between 100 miles (160 kilometers) and thousands of miles
- **HEIGHT:** 45 feet (14 meters)
- **MATERIALS:** Earth and rock

More than a thousand years ago, in the lush green rainforest of Nigeria, the Yoruba People built a protective wall with a moat running alongside it. The jungle eventually grew over the wall and left it all but invisible until recently. The Yoruba People built the defense system—now known as Sungbo's Eredo—to encircle and protect their kingdom. Scientists estimate the builders used more than 123 million cubic feet (3.5 million cubic meters) of rock and earth—more than the material used in the Great Pyramid of Cheops in Egypt! The wall may also have been stronger because the damp jungle soil and clay made a tougher mix. Some archaeologists believe the Eredo wall makers purposefully dug down until they reached groundwater, which guaranteed the moat would fill with water and become a swampy barrier beside the wall. Though it was forgotten for centuries and overgrown by the bright-green trees and vines of the rainforest, a lot of the wall is still standing today. It's become a source of national pride and tourism for Nigeria. And it has sparked questions about who commissioned the building of the wall in the first place.

The Queen of Sheba?

The Ijebu people, who are part of the broader group of Yoruba People, claim the wall was built to honor the memory of a wealthy noblewoman named Oloye Bilikisu Sungbo, who always wanted to keep enemies out and keep the Ijebu kingdom unified. Some people in Nigeria and beyond believe Sungbo was the legendary Queen of Sheba, who is named in the **Bible** and referred to in the **Koran**. The Queen of Sheba is said to have married King Solomon and may have established Jewish settlements in Ethiopia. Archaeologists studying Sungbo's Eredo say that this and many other questions need more study. The Nigerian government has applied to have the ancient wall declared a UNESCO World Heritage site, and in 2021 the US Mission in Nigeria donated $400,000 for the mapping and preservation of the wall.

KUÉLAP

- *BUILT: c. 900–1100*
- *LENGTH: About 1900 feet (580 meters) • WIDTH: Up to 360 feet (110 meters)*
- *HEIGHT: Up to 65 feet (20 meters) • MATERIAL: Limestone*

In South America, the Chachapoya People built strong stone walls to defend themselves more than a thousand years ago. They lived on the eastern slopes of the Andes Mountains, high above the Amazon rainforest in what is now Peru, and were known to the neighboring Inca people as Warriors of the Clouds. Sometime between 900 and 1100 they built an impressive city in the sky, called Kuélap, on a mountaintop more than 9,800 feet (3,000 meters) above sea level, overlooking the Utcubamba River valley. The Chachapoyas cut limestone into large blocks—some weighing as much as 3 tons (2.72 metric tons)—and used them to build walls to form an area the shape of a **trapezoid**.

The walls are still standing today and are connected to a watchtower that once defended Kuélap from attack and helped make it the center of Chachapoya civilization, where government, military and religious buildings were based. The walls also protected 420 circular stone houses. Warriors, farmers and many other people lived inside the walls. At its peak Kuélap may have been home to more than 5,000 people. Kuélap thrived for hundreds of years, but the neighboring Inca Empire finally conquered the city around the year 1470—about 100 years before the Spanish conquered the Incas.

The Inca also built a walled fortress of their own. It was an imposing fortress just north of their capital city, Cusco. Construction started in the 1400s, under Emperor Pachacuti. The fortress was called Sacsayhuamán, which means "where the falcon or hawk is satisfied" in the Quechua language. It was built with huge dry stones, cut carefully so they would hold together with no mortar. Sacsayhuamán was built in the clouds—at an altitude of more than 12,000 feet (3,700 meters). The giant stones were cut from a type of volcanic rock called andesite. Some weigh almost 200 tons (180 metric tons) and are considered some of the largest stones ever cut in the Americas before the arrival of Europeans. Despite their size, the stones were cut extremely carefully, so that there are few, if any, gaps. In fact, many visitors have noticed they can't even slide a piece of paper between the blocks! In addition, many blocks were cut with rounded edges, which makes them cling to each other even more. This may have helped the walls of Sacsayhuamán remain standing through major earthquakes, which happen there once or twice a century.

TLAXCALA DEFENSIVE WALLS

In the 15th century, in modern-day Mexico, the Tlaxcalan people built defensive walls to guard against their powerful neighbors, the Aztecs. The two **Indigenous** groups fought many wars with each other before the Spanish colonized Mexico, but the powerful Aztecs never conquered Tlaxcala. According to a letter from Spanish conquistador Hernán Cortés, the Spanish arrived in 1519 and made their way inland from the coast. They started marching up the valley that led to the Tlaxcala people, when they "found a great wall of dry stones, about nine feet high, which crossed the whole valley from one mountain to the other; it was twenty feet thick, and had a stone parapet, a foot and a half broad on the top so that no one could fight from above," said Cortés.

The walls had kept the Aztecs out, but Spanish soldiers fought their way into Tlaxcalan territory. Tens of thousands of Tlaxcalan warriors fought against the Spanish, and many were killed in the battles. Eventually the Tlaxcalan king Xīcohtēncatl the Younger invited the Spanish **conquistador** Hernán Cortés to his capital, where he stayed for 20 days. The two leaders agreed they would form an alliance against the Aztecs. When Cortés left, his soldiers were joined by 6,000 Tlaxcalan warriors who marched to the Aztec capital, Tenochtitlan, and eventually defeated the Aztecs.

This drawing from the 16th century shows the Tlaxcalan king Xīcohtēncatl the Younger coming to an agreement with the Spanish invader Hernán Cortés.
DIEGO MUNOZ DE CAMARGO/ WIKIMEDIA COMMONS/PUBLIC DOMAIN

THE GREAT WALL OF INDIA
- **BUILT:** *15th century* • **LENGTH:** *23 miles (37 kilometers)*
- **HEIGHT:** *15 to 25 feet (4 to 7 meters)* • **WIDTH:** *Up to 15 feet (4.5 meters)*
- **MATERIAL:** *Stone*

India also has many walls. The state of Rajasthan is famous for its hill forts. More than 100 still stand today. Some are more than 1,000 years old. Many are surrounded by defensive walls that were designed to protect not only the people inside but also temples, courtyards and gardens.

The Kumbhalgarh fortress, near the city of Udaipur, is surrounded by one of the longest walls in the world, known to many as the Great Wall of India. The fortress was built in the 15th century by Rana Kumbha (Kumbhakarna Singh), who was the ruler of the Mewar kingdom in India. The fort wall is built to take advantage of its natural surroundings. It is surrounded by 13 mountain peaks and has seven giant gates as well as huge watchtowers. Over the centuries it proved to be safe, and even protected Udai Singh—the local king who was still just a baby—from the battles being fought outside the fort wall.

MAGINOT LINE

• BUILT: 1928 • LENGTH: 280 miles (450 kilometers)
• LOCATION: France–Germany border • MATERIALS: Reinforced concrete and steel

The French government built one of the most formidable collection of walls in the 1930s. The Maginot Line was a series of defenses that included underground bunkers, minefields, fortresses and gun batteries. It was built with reinforced concrete and 55 million tons (50 million metric tons) of steel, buried deep below the surface along France's border with Germany. It was made with World War I still fresh in the memory of millions of people and named after a French politician, André Maginot, who had been so seriously injured in that war that he walked on crutches for the rest of his life. In the 1920s Maginot convinced the French government to spend a fortune on border defenses against Germany—the equivalent of more than US$9 billion today.

Blitzkrieg

Despite all that money, the walls did not work. They were designed to stop the slower methods of fighting—mostly trench warfare—that were typical of World War I. But when Nazi Germany invaded France in 1940, it adopted a much different style of fighting, called blitzkrieg—they attacked with armored tanks and aircraft. Instead of trying to fight their way through the Maginot Line, the Nazis went around it, punching through the Ardennes forests in Belgium. They crossed into France quickly, behind the Maginot Line, and surrounded British and French armies, pushing some to the Atlantic coast and capturing upward of a half million more soldiers. The Nazis then captured Paris, occupying much of France for another five years.

French Army officers stand on top of a fort on the Maginot Line and look toward Germany, in 1939. Nazi forces would soon overwhelm the Maginot Line and occupy much of France the following year.
KEYSTONE/GETTY IMAGES

Walls of Jericho
8300 BCE

Rabbit-Proof Fence
1901–1907

Dingo Fence
1880–1885

Five

TO CONTROL NATURE

Most walls are built with people in mind, but others are designed to control nature. Some stop animals from going where they are not wanted. Others stop water from flowing where it shouldn't. And other barriers protect plant life in precisely the places we do want it to grow.

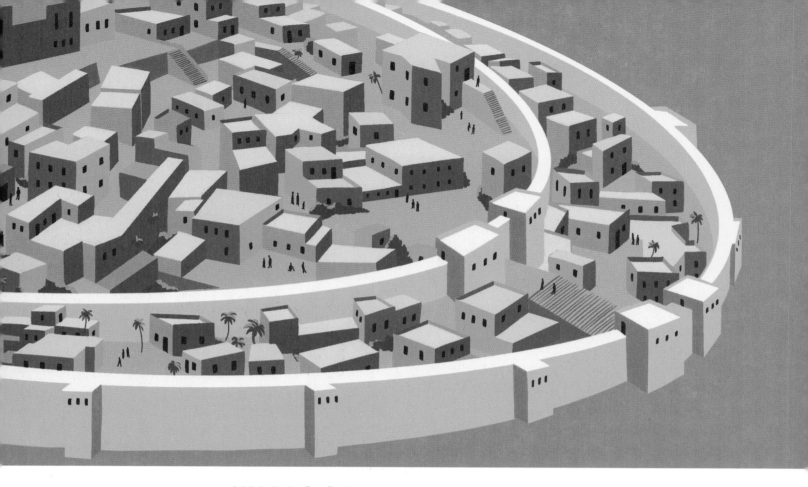

WALLS OF JERICHO

- **BUILT:** *8300 BCE* · **WIDTH:** *About 6 feet (2 meters)*
- **HEIGHT:** *About 12 feet (4 meters)* · **MATERIALS:** *Earth and stone*

It's difficult to say for sure where humans first built walls because many early structures have disappeared over the centuries—they've fallen down, been torn down or sunk slowly into the earth. The oldest we know about are the stone walls of Jericho, which archaeologists have unearthed at Tell es-Sultan—also called Tel Jericho—in the West Bank. The ancient walls were mentioned in biblical stories about the Battle of Jericho, when the Israelites crossed the Jordan River to enter Canaan and attacked the city of Jericho. Because they're so old, archaeologists don't know exactly why the walls were built. They may have been designed to protect the people of Jericho from enemy attacks. But some archaeologists believe they were built to protect Jericho's people from a natural attack—namely, floods. The River Jordan is very close to the walls and has flooded many times.

Builders' Legacy

The walls were built around 8300 BCE, not long after the town was established. Hundreds of people—maybe thousands—lived in houses made from mud bricks. Thumbprints from builders can still be seen in the bricks more than 10,000 years later! But the walls that were built around the houses was made completely of heavy stones, brought down to the town from the surrounding hills. The ditch beside the walls was cut into solid **bedrock** and would have taken a huge effort to dig.

RABBIT-PROOF FENCE

- *BUILT: 1901–1907*
- *LENGTH OF NO. 1 FENCE: 1,133 miles (1,824 kilometers).*
- *TOTAL LENGTH OF ALL THREE FENCES: 2,023 miles (3,256 kilometers)*
- *HEIGHT: 3 feet, 7 inches (1.1 meters) • MATERIALS: Iron, wood and wire mesh*

In Australia the barriers are less impressive in height and width but are unbelievably long! And in most cases they were built to stop animals from moving around. The Indigenous people of Australia have lived on the continent for tens of thousands of years. When British settlers arrived in 1788, they brought some of their animals with them, like cats, goats, foxes and rabbits. The first rabbits to arrive likely didn't multiply in number because they were bred for food and kept in cages. But in 1859 a man named Thomas Austin imported 24 wild rabbits from England and released them into the wild so his guests would have something to hunt. They may have shot a few, but many more rabbits survived. And they spread across Australia quickly. With almost no **predators** to stop them, the furry immigrants grazed on all sorts of native flowers and grasses and multiplied

every day. There were soon millions of rabbits—all of them descendants of those 24 rabbits that Austin imported—eating up most of the grass, which also led to **erosion** of the soil.

Riled Up over Rabbits

Farmers were desperate to keep rabbits off their property, so they turned to fences. Some of the first fences were actually stone walls, but those weren't very effective because the rabbits could dig under them or squeeze through gaps between the stones. In some cases, the rabbits ended up living in those gaps. Next the farmers tried long rows of wooden boards, called bunny boards. But the wood rotted quickly, and most farmers started using wire. In the 1860s they built long animal-exclusion fences around their farms, constructed of wooden posts joined by wire mesh and with openings

ANIMAL FENCE-BUILDERS

While the Rabbit-Proof Fence was built to keep certain animals out of Western Australia, the people who built it needed other types of animals to help with the work. The 120 humans who built the No. 1 Fence were helped by an army of animals that were also species introduced to Australia. Forty-one donkeys, 210 horses and 350 camels worked on the fence. The camels were especially useful in the dry deserts of Western Australia because they can survive for days without drinking any water while also carrying heavy loads. Some historians suggested the fence would not have been finished when it was without the help of camels.

too small for most animals to pass through. Australia's territories built even longer rabbit fences, but in many cases they found that the rabbits were managing to hop across to the other side before the fence was even finished.

By 1890 the rabbits had spread all the way to Australia's west coast. The colonial government of Western Australia sent a surveyor east in 1896, to study the rabbit population. When Arthur Mason returned, he suggested Western Australia should build a series of long fences to stop more rabbits from migrating. In 1901 Western Australia joined the new country of Australia, and one of its first decisions was to build the No. 1 Fence, a barrier running across the state. It was the first of three long fences, which would together be known as the Rabbit-Proof Fence, and eventually the State Barrier Fence of Western Australia.

A Long, Long, Long Job

Construction started within months, but it took six years to complete because the fences were so long. They stretched from the south coast in a long line north to the northwest coast of Australia. No. 1 Fence was the longest unbroken fence in the world at that time. The fence posts were mostly made of wood, though some were made of iron. They were spaced roughly 12 feet apart (3.7 meters) and stood 3 feet (0.9 meters) above ground. Wire mesh—Australians call it netting— was added to the bottom, extending 6 inches (15 centimeters) below ground to prevent animals from digging under the fence. The State Barrier Fence of Western Australia was later made taller to keep dingoes and foxes out.

Pest-exclusion fences have had mixed results. They helped many farmers protect their livestock for many years, and scientists say they have provided critical protection for endangered birds, reptiles and small mammals. But they didn't control the rabbits. Australia's wild rabbits have caused ecological devastation, and their population has been estimated to be as high as 200 million!

A section of the Rabbit-Proof Fence in the Gascoyne region of Western Australia. It is illegal for members of the public to travel on the track that runs beside the fence. The road is reserved for the vehicles of people who work on the fence and with wildlife. There are security cameras along the fence, and anyone caught driving there illegally could be fined up to $10,000.
STEVE ROGERS/GETTY IMAGES

DINGO FENCE

- *BUILT: 1880–1885* - *LENGTH: 3,488 miles (5,614 kilometers)*
- *HEIGHT: 6 feet (1.8 meters)* - *AUSTRALIAN STATES IT PASSES THROUGH: 3*

Like the State Barrier Fence of Western Australia, a long fence in southeast Australia was constructed to keep out foxes and dingoes. The longest one is now known as the dingo fence. It was built in the 1880s, and it stretches an incredible distance across southeastern Australia. The fence was designed to protect flocks of sheep from dingoes, which are a type of wild dog that has lived on the Australian continent for thousands of years. Dingoes hunt all sorts of animals, including kangaroos, wallabies, rabbits, rats and birds. They will also hunt sheep, lambs in particular. So farmers and state governments built new fences and linked them with many of the old fences that were built in the 1800s.

Fence Patrol

It takes a lot of work to look after such a long fence. It requires people to patrol it every day. In the early days, patrollers rode camels to check for damage and repair it. Now they drive pickup trucks—called utes by Australians. They find a lot of damage. Dingoes dig under the fence, and some kangaroos slam themselves into it, hoping to smash through to the other side for better grazing. The fence includes a series of gates to allow farm vehicles through. Where major roads cross the fence, a cattle grid is installed on the road surface to prevent animals from crossing. Other than that, the fence is pretty simple—wooden posts linked together with wire mesh. Some stretches are lit by fluorescent lights, alternating between white light and red. They're powered by solar panels that capture the power from Australia's sunny skies.

The dingo fence has been called "the world's largest ecological field experiment" because it divides Australia into two giant ecosystems—one with tens of thousands of dingoes, the other with almost none. Dingoes are the last large predator left in Australia, and the dingo fence has let scientists test how dingoes threaten the reptiles, wallabies and other animals they hunt. It was assumed for a long time that dingoes threaten small-animal populations, but recent research suggests it might be the opposite. This may be because the dingoes reduce the number of foxes, which live on both sides of the fence, and are also a predator of wallabies and reptiles. Plant life is also more diverse on the side with the dingoes, probably because there are fewer kangaroos to graze on the grasses when there are dingoes to hunt them.

Korean Demilitarized Zone
1953

Northern Ireland Peace Walls
1969-present

Vietnam Veterans Memorial
1982

Six

TO KEEP TWO SIDES APART

When a war or other violent conflict comes to an end, a barrier can be a useful thing to build between sides, but sometimes that barrier can cause more problems than it solves. Sometimes it's a sturdy wall of steel or concrete. Other times the barrier isn't a physical structure—it's simply a no-go zone that's off-limits to people on either side.

Walled Neighborhoods of Brazil
c. 1970s

The DMZ also sits between two dams. In 1986—two years before South Korea hosted the Olympics—North Korea started building the large Imnam Dam on the Bukhan River, which flows south. Military leaders in South Korea worried their northern neighbors might choose to release a huge amount of water to flood South Korea. So they began work on their own dam, 22 miles (35 kilometers) farther south of the Imnam Dam. They called it the Peace Dam and hoped it would protect people in the south from flooding. Work stalled on the dam for years, but it was finally finished in 2005. It stands 410 feet (125 meters) high and 1,971 feet (601 meters) wide. Unlike most dams, it does not contain a large reservoir of water behind it. Its only purpose is to prevent a flood from the other side of the DMZ. The *New York Times* called the giant dam a "$429 million monument to the politics on the divided peninsula."

KOREAN DEMILITARIZED ZONE

- *ESTABLISHED: 1953* - *LENGTH: 150 miles (240 kilometers)*
- *WIDTH: 2.5 miles (4 kilometers)*

The Korean Peninsula, in East Asia, was a unified kingdom for hundreds of years. It was split into North and South Korea after World War II. Then North Korea invaded the south in 1950, and the fighting continued for three years. When the fighting finally stopped, 2.5 million people had died and the two countries were more divided than ever. This devastating war left much of the country in rubble and two countries separated by a long strip of land along the 38th parallel, called the Korean Demilitarized Zone (DMZ). The DMZ is not a traditional wall of steel or stone, but a long thin strip of land without people.

Big Armies on Both Sides

Thousands of soldiers stand guard on either side of the DMZ, including more than 30,000 members of the American military on the south side. North Korea has many soldiers, tanks and giant rocket launchers that can fire deadly missiles a long way into South Korea, including the country's capital, Seoul, which is just 25 miles (40 kilometers) south of the DMZ. The only section of the border where South Koreans can stand face-to-face with North Koreans is a place called the Joint Security Area, which is overseen by the United Nations. Guards from each country stand side by side on either side of the border line. South Korean guards must have a black belt in tae kwon do to work at this important post. North Korea has tried to tunnel under the DMZ at least four times. In 1990, under the town of Haean, a tunnel six feet, six inches (two meters) high was discovered before North Korea could finish digging.

NORTHERN IRELAND PEACE WALLS

· **BUILT:** *1969–present* · **LENGTH:** *A few hundred feet to 3 miles (5 kilometers)*
· **HEIGHT:** *Up to 25 feet (8 meters)* · **MATERIALS:** *Brick, iron and steel*

Northern Ireland has been divided for many years between Protestants, who want to remain a part of the United Kingdom of Great Britain and Northern Ireland, and **Catholic**s, who want to leave Britain and join the Republic of Ireland. While most people in Northern Ireland disagreed peacefully, others resorted to violence. Members of both sides were the victims of bombings, shootings and kidnappings. In total more than 3,600 people died between 1968 and 1998. Unlike two different countries at war, the opposing sides lived side by side, with many Catholic neighborhoods standing across the street from **Protestant** ones. In response, the government in Northern Ireland built a series of separation barriers, known to many as peace walls. Some were erected in the 1920s and 1930s, but most were

built in the 1960s, when an era known as the Troubles began. Most were built in the capital city of Belfast, though some went up in towns like Derry, Portadown and Lurgan. The solid walls were built with gates that police could open during the day and lock shut at night.

Still Standing

The Troubles ended officially in 1998, with the signing of the Good Friday Agreement, but the walls still remained. Twenty years after the peace accord was signed, many walls had grown longer and higher. While Northern Ireland committed to remove all barriers by 2023, several remain. Many people in Northern Ireland still hope that all the walls will come down soon.

An aerial view of the Belfast peace walls, which divide Catholic and Protestant communities. Some residents of Belfast would like to tear the walls down, but more than 50 years after they were first erected, progress toward this goal has been slow.
TCROWEPHOTO/GETTY IMAGES

ART ON A DANGEROUS LINE

The peace walls have proved a tempting target for artists. Many are covered by colorful murals made up of images, slogans and paintings. Some of those paintings depict people who died in the Troubles. Others show the flags that claim the loyalties of the people on either side. Others urge all residents of Northern Ireland to move past old animosities and live in peace. And some even urge the tearing down of the walls on which they're painted, such as the message in big capital letters that reads *BRING DOWN THE WALLS.*

WALLED NEIGHBORHOODS OF BRAZIL

Many wealthy people in Brazil have moved into gated communities surrounded by walls. As the country's big cities have grown in size over the last 30 years, with many people coming to the cities in search of work, crime has increased as well. A lot of rich Brazilians concerned about crime choose to buy nice big houses in the growing number of gated communities. The high walls are designed to keep out anyone who doesn't live in the community. People who live there have to enter through the gates, where guards who work for the owners check the identification of everyone who wants to go inside.

Safe...But Is It Fair?

Many people who live inside gated communities say they feel much safer living behind the walls, and an awful lot of Brazilians have chosen to live this way. A 2011 study estimated there were one million homes in gated communities in Brazil. But some people question whether it is fair to leave many poor and vulnerable people without the same protection. Although Brazil has certainly seen its more fortunate residents build

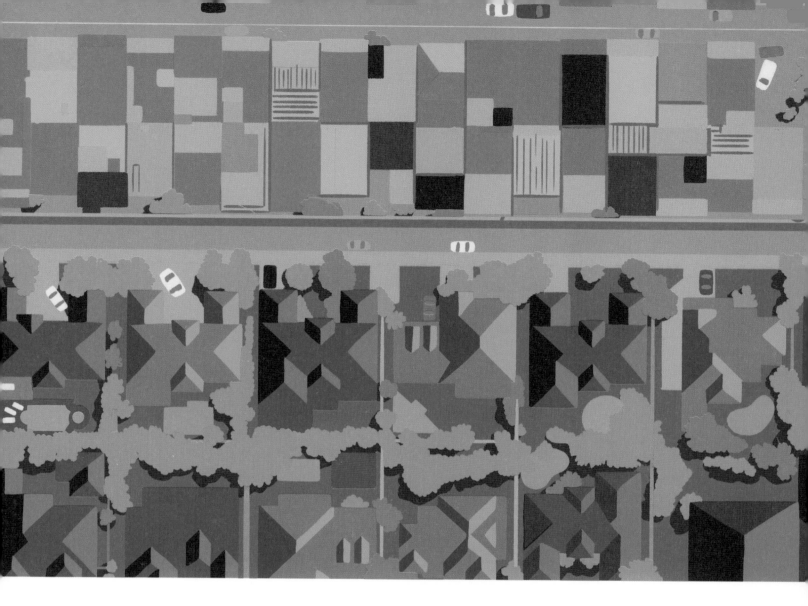

more and more communities that are surrounded and protected by walls, it is not the only country to do so. South American neighbors Argentina and Ecuador also have protected enclaves. Around the world, dozens of other countries have too—Canada, China, Russia, Saudi Arabia, Turkey, the United States and at least a dozen more have seen citizens with more money build barriers in the name of safety.

Separating Haves and Have-Nots

As we've seen, gated communities separate the rich from the poor. Some Brazilian cities have also erected concrete walls around some of its poorest neighborhoods to stop them from growing even larger. *Favelas*, or shantytowns, are growing communities of shacks and other simple homes that fill up with poor people looking for jobs and a better life in the city. But some of those poor neighborhoods are now huge—Rocinha has more than 180,000 people!—and officials in Rio de Janeiro have tried to stop them from growing even bigger. They've built walls they say will protect the lush green forest that surrounds the city, well known as a tourism destination. But some Brazilians worry that building more walls will only widen the divide between the country's rich and poor.

VIETNAM VETERANS MEMORIAL

• BUILT: 1982 • LENGTH: 493 feet (150 meters) • LOCATION: Washington, DC
• MATERIAL: Polished black granite

Americans started discussing the need for a public memorial a few years after the Vietnam War ended. So a contest was held to design a memorial that would remember the people who had lost their lives but not comment on "the rightness, wrongness or motivation" of American involvement in the war. The judges had to consider 1,422 entries. It was a difficult task, but in the end they chose a design submitted by a 21-year-old student at Yale University, named Maya Lin. One of Lin's professors had challenged his students to enter the contest. When Lin visited the Washington park where the memorial would be located, she was impressed by the beauty of the natural surroundings. "I didn't want to destroy a living park," she said. "You use the landscape, you don't fight with it." Lin imagined "taking a knife and cutting into the earth, opening it up, and with the passage of time, that initial violence and pain would heal."

When the **Vietnam War** ended in 1975, more than two million people had been killed in the fighting. The vast majority of victims were Vietnamese, but the war had caused years of pain and division in the United States as well. While some Americans thought their government was right to send soldiers across the Pacific Ocean, others opposed the war. While there was no wall standing between them, millions of Americans were divided by their opinions on the Vietnam War. But an American **veteran** named Jan Scruggs had a dream for a memorial wall that would eventually bring people together. The memorial is actually two separate walls sunken into the ground, with earth piled behind them. They sit next to each other, at an angle, to form a V shape. They rise up to 10 feet (3 meters) where they meet and drop gradually by a total

of 8 inches (20 centimeters) at both ends. The walls are engraved with the names of the more than 58,000 Americans who served and died in the war. The memorial has become a place for their loved ones to meet and remember them, and many leave flags and flowers in memory of their friends and family members whose names are listed on the wall.

Like the war, Maya Lin's design was controversial. Some veterans thought the dark color and low height made it look like it was trying to hide, as if the wall was communicating that veterans should feel ashamed for having served in the military. But millions of veterans visited the wall and were brought to tears seeing the names of their families and friends. With the passage of time, Lin's memorial wall has become an important part of the American landscape.

At 555 feet (169 meters) high, the Washington Monument looms over the Vietnam Veterans Memorial. Around three million people visit the memorial wall every year.
RUDY SULGAN/GETTY IMAGES

Lugo
263–276

Dubrovnik
c. 1300–1500

The City Walls of
Constantinople
c. 300–500

Colonial Walls in Quebec
1608–1871

Seven

TO PROTECT THE CITY

While some ancient empires built long walls across the countryside, others built shorter stone walls around cities. Many still stand, though most of the cities have now grown beyond them. Ávila and Segovia in Spain, Carcassonne in France and York in England are all excellent examples of cities that grew wealthy behind solid walls.

Some walls are built inside large cities to protect a key institution inside it. The Roman Catholic Church is based in Vatican City, which is surrounded by the much larger city of Rome. Despite standing in the middle of the Italian capital, Vatican City is considered a sovereign territory and is the smallest independent state in the world, based on both land size and population. The Vatican is just 121 acres (49 hectares), with fewer than 1,000 people. But the small population is surrounded by a large stone wall. It stands between most of the Vatican and the rest of Rome, though it does not surround the Vatican completely. The first wall was built in the 850s, not long after Saracen raiders attacked the Vatican. Pope Leo IV decided a strong wall was needed to guard against future attacks. The wall still stands, but the big gates have been open for a long time, and every year millions of visitors simply walk through them to visit the Vatican's museums or St. Peter's Basilica church.

DUBROVNIK

- **BUILT:** *c. 1300–1500* • **LENGTH:** *6,360 feet (1,940 meters)*
- **HEIGHT:** *Up to 82 feet (25 meters)* • **MATERIAL:** *Limestone*
- **CANNONS ALONG WALL:** *120*

One of the most stunning examples of a walled city is Dubrovnik, in southern Croatia. The city was built on a rocky stretch of coastline on the Adriatic Sea. It's surrounded by magnificent stone walls built more than 500 years ago. They were so effective that they helped the independent Republic of Ragusa, based in Dubrovnik, last for centuries.

Not Just the Middle Ages

Dubrovnik's walls have helped city residents defend themselves from enemies as recently as the 1990s. The Yugoslav People's Army attacked Dubrovnik during the Croatian War of Independence in 1991. They first attacked from the sea, then fired rockets and mortars from neighboring hills. Refugees poured into the Old Town, hoping they would be safer behind the walls. Not everyone was. Some civilians were killed, and the walls and many old buildings were heavily damaged. The American Institute of Architects condemned the bombardment of the city's Old Town. Fierce fighting continued into the following year, but the Croatian military kept the Yugoslav People's Army out, thanks in part to the ancient walls.

SERVIAN WALL

- *BUILT: c. 400 BCE*
- *LENGTH: 6.8 miles (11 kilometers)*
- *HEIGHT: 33 feet (10 meters)*
- *WIDTH: 12 feet (3.6 meters)*
- *GATES THROUGH WALL: 16*

The Roman Empire built a lot of walls. One of the most important was the Servian Wall around the city of Rome. Named after the sixth Roman king, Servius Tullius, it was built from tuff, a type of solid rock that's formed from the ash that's blown out of a volcano. The Servian Wall was a strong defense, but it couldn't contain the growing city. As the empire expanded, Rome eventually grew past the walls. By the 3rd century BCE, tribes from northern Europe were attacking the great city, and Emperor Aurelian ordered the construction of a bigger set of walls—called the Aurelian Walls, of course!—to protect more of the city.

LUGO

- *BUILT: 263–276*
- *LENGTH: 6,946 feet (2,117 meters)*
- *HEIGHT: 33–49 feet (10–15 meters)*
- *TOWERS ALONG WALL: 71*
- *MATERIAL: Stone*

The only city in the world that still has a completely intact Roman wall surrounding it is Lugo, in the autonomous Spanish region of Galicia. The Romans captured the town and named it Lucus Augusti around 15 BCE, and the small city became one of two capitals of the Roman province of Gallaecia. Over the years Lugo was attacked many times, so the Romans built the wall to prevent invasions from outsiders. The Suevi, Visigoths, Moors and Normans all attacked in the years that followed. But the Roman wall of Lugo has remained for more than 1,700 years and is now recognized as a World Heritage site.

Several stretches of the Servian Wall in Rome are still standing. This segment is close to Roma Termini, the city's busiest railway station, which was built over parts of the wall. There's even a section of the original wall located in a McDonald's restaurant inside the station!

SALVATORE FALCO/WIKIMEDIA COMMONS/CC SA 1.0

A GOVERNMENT FORTRESS

The government buildings of Russia also stand behind a thick barrier, in the middle of Moscow. The Kremlin is a fortress surrounded by a wall with a series of towers and gates running along it, and more than 1,000 notched "teeth" jutting up from its top. The current wall was designed by Italian architects in the 1600s. But it isn't the first wall to surround the Kremlin. A wooden wall was erected in the 1100s, when Moscow was first established. Then in the 1300s, limestone was used to build the first stone wall there—much of it pulled to Moscow over the snow on sleds. Now Moscow has spread many miles past the Kremlin walls, and they protect only the most important buildings of Russia's government.

THE CITY WALLS OF CONSTANTINOPLE

- **BUILT:** *c. 300–500* · **OUTER WALL HEIGHT:** *39 feet (12 meters)*
- **WIDTH:** *14–19 feet (4.5–6 meters)*
- **LENGTH:** *Theodosian Walls stretch 3.5 miles (5.7 kilometers)*
- **MATERIALS:** *Limestone, red brick and mortared rubble*

Despite its strong walls, Rome faced many challenges, including disease, civil war and invasions. So the Roman Empire moved much of its focus to the ancient city of Byzantium (now Istanbul, Turkey). Emperor Constantine renamed the city New Rome in 324 and declared it the new capital of the Roman Empire. Six years later the city was renamed Constantinople. In the centuries that followed, it became the largest and richest city in Europe. The city had already had strong stone walls for many years. But Constantine started a massive project to build the last massive fortification of antiquity that would eventually grow into one of the most complex systems of defensive walls ever built.

Theodosian Walls

In the fifth century, construction started on the double Theodosian Walls to protect the city from both land and sea. The taller inner wall included 96 towers, while the outer wall was thinner and less than half its height. But the combination of the two walls and an outside moat proved impossible for enemies to cross for hundreds of years. Perhaps the biggest challenge for Constantinople's walls over those years

came from earthquakes. Several shakers caused considerable damage to both towers and the wall itself. But the structure was such a key part of Constantinople's security that repairing them was a priority.

Walls to Last a Thousand Years

Constantinople sat in a very strategic place, on the Bosphorus—a strait of water that forms the continental boundary between Europe and Asia. Over the centuries many armies tried and failed to conquer Constantinople and the Byzantine Empire, as the Eastern Roman Empire became known. But the walls were not breached until 1453—more than a thousand years after they were first built—when the Ottomans used their greater numbers in a six-week siege to capture Constantinople. When the walls were finally overcome, the empire fell.

Many stretches of the Theodosian Walls in Istanbul still stand today, including many towers. A great number of tourists visit the walls to see and touch the historic fortification.
SALVATOR BARKI/GETTY IMAGES

COLONIAL WALLS IN QUEBEC

- **BUILT:** 1608–1871 · **LENGTH:** 2.9 miles (4.6 kilometers)
- **WIDTH OF RAMPARTS AND DITCHES:** 240 feet (73 meters)
- **MATERIALS:** Green sandstone and wood

One of four main city gates built into the wall around Old Quebec City. The gates served as control points where soldiers could check people coming in and out of the city. They could also be closed and barricaded to keep enemies out.
DANIELA DUNCAN/GETTY IMAGES

In 1608 French explorer Samuel de Champlain established a trading post on a rocky ***promontory*** overlooking what he called "the River of Canada." The post would later become Quebec City. The town stood in a commanding position, high above the river on top of a 300-foot (90-meter) cliff, making it extremely difficult for invading soldiers to capture. At first the French relied on the cliffs and modest defenses, but when the British conquered the settlement of Port Royal in the French colony of Acadia in 1690, they decided Quebec City needed much stronger defensive walls to guard against invasion along the west side of the town— the only side not protected by cliffs. They built large stone ***ramparts*** and dug ditches beside the wall to create a giant slope— called a glacis—that concealed the wall from the enemy's view.

The British Are Coming

When Britain and France went to war in the 1750s, the British decided they would try to capture the fortress city. In 1759 British soldiers sailed upstream from Quebec City and climbed up a cliff to assemble outside the city wall, on a field called the Plains of Abraham. When the French leader, Louis-Joseph de Montcalm, learned of their arrival, he sent French soldiers outside the city walls to fight. Many soldiers died on both sides, including Montcalm and the British major general, James Wolfe. After five days of fighting outside the walls, the few surviving French soldiers inside the city surrendered to the British.

The Americans Are Coming

Quebec City's mighty walls would help the British 15 years later, at the start of the American War of Independence, when American forces laid siege to Quebec. Once again the walls let British soldiers hang on until their ships returned in the spring. The British were so impressed with the walls that they built more. In the 1820s they built a walled fortress called the ***Citadel*** inside the city walls, meant to protect them from foreign troops and even from the French inhabitants of Quebec City if they decided to revolt.

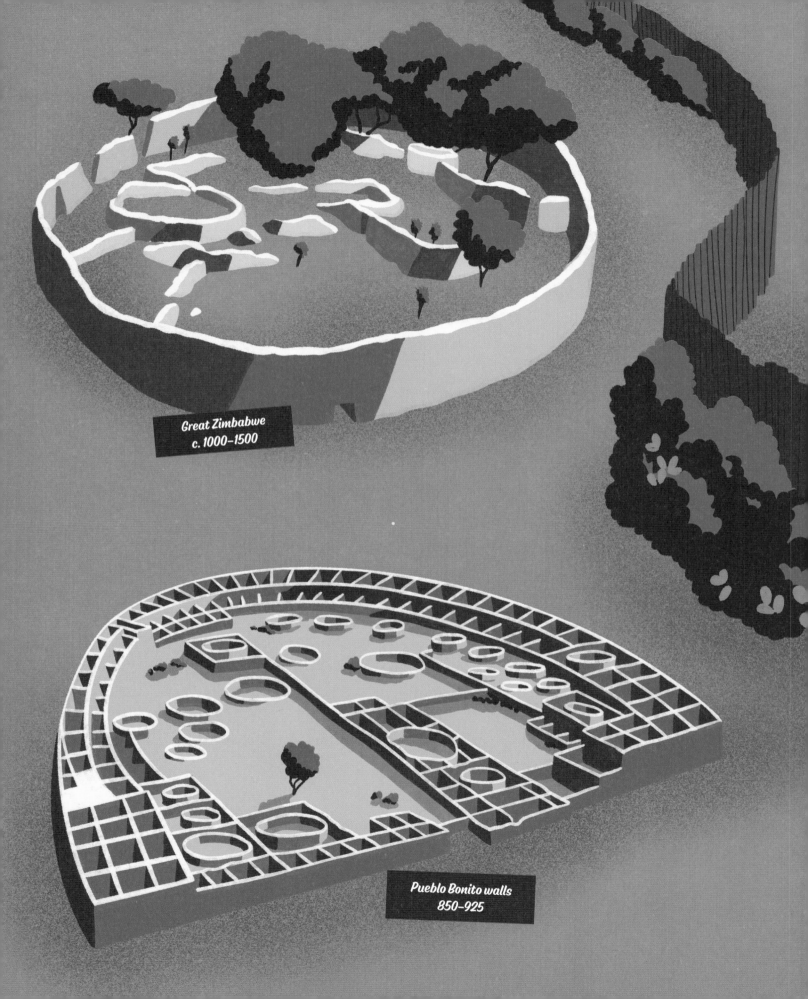

Great Zimbabwe
c. 1000–1500

Pueblo Bonito walls
850–925

Eight

TO MAKE MONEY

Most walls were built to control the movement of people, but some were built specifically to collect money from those people that carry it with them. Some walls helped in the collection of taxes. Others helped traders and merchants protect their money from thieves. In that sense, the walls paid for themselves. But at least one wall was far too costly to the people who had to cross it.

GREAT ZIMBABWE

- *BUILT: c. 1000–1500* • *LENGTH: 820 feet (250 meters)*
- *HEIGHT: Up to 32 feet (9.7 meters)* • *MATERIAL: Stone*

Hundreds of years ago in southeastern Africa, the Shona People grew the Kingdom of Zimbabwe into a successful trading empire. Their capital was located near the modern city of Masvingo and was occupied from the 11th to the 15th century. *Zimbabwe* is the Shona word for "stone houses," and it was a fitting name for the walled capital city. The first buildings were built there in a hill complex around 900. Then a strong rock wall was built around a lower section of the complex, now known as the Great Enclosure. Another wall was built on the inside of those walls and connected to a tower 33 feet (10 meters) high.

Why Build It?

Archaeologists are not sure exactly what the tower was used for. Was it a large storage facility for grain? Or perhaps a royal residence? Whatever the specific use, it's clear the city was an important center of commerce. The Great Zimbabwe Empire controlled trade along Africa's east coast, and many items found in what was known as Great Zimbabwe attest to that fact— Arab coins, for example, and pottery from as far away as China. Nearby ruins show there were many mud-brick houses near the walls, and as many as 20,000 people could have lived there. The Shona People eventually left, though. By the 15th century, Great Zimbabwe was largely abandoned.

THE GREAT HEDGE OF INDIA

- *GROWN: c. 1840–1880*
- *LENGTH: Between 411 miles (661 kilometers) and 1,520 miles (2,446 kilometers)*
- *HEIGHT: Up to 12 feet (4 meters)* • *WIDTH: 14 feet (5 meters)*
- *MATERIALS: Bamboo, Indian plum, prickly pear and other plants*

While most barriers are built, one was grown. In the 1800s British colonial rulers planted and maintained a wall of bushes that stretched across much of India. The living wall formed part of the longer Inland Customs Line that stretched 2,500 miles (4,000 kilometers) from the western Himalayan mountains across India to the Bay of Bengal. The hedge was first made of dead spiky bushes, like the Indian plum, which has long thorns that sting the skin of people or animals who are pricked. In some dry areas, where nothing else would grow, a type of cactus called a prickly pear was planted. In wetter stretches, bamboo was used. The hedge was cared for by as many as 12,000 people and lasted for about 50 years, even though it faced many threats, including ants, locusts, rats, decay and strong winds, all of which could have destroyed it. But this hedge was not a gardening wonder—it served a very practical purpose for British colonial rulers. It helped them collect money in the form of a salt tax, which gave the hedge its other common name—the Indian Salt Hedge. A long road ran beside the hedge, which helped customs officials make sure no one took salt across or through the hedge without paying taxes.

The Most "Inhuman" Tax

The tax was essentially a price that anyone transporting salt across India from the Punjab region, where it was produced, had to pay. The British collected millions of *rupees* from the Indian people through the salt tax. But it was an expensive fee for one of the essential elements of life, and millions of poor Indians had to pay, even during famines when many were starving and could not afford food. Mahatma Gandhi, the leader of India's independence movement, called it "the most inhuman poll tax that ingenuity of man can devise."

Prickly pear cactus like this was one of the main plants that formed the Great Hedge of India. The hardy cactus has been used for centuries as a natural fence for grazing animals in many arid regions around the world. British rulers in India used it to help them herd people and collect taxes.
IAISI/GETTY IMAGES

WHY TAX SALT?

It may seem strange today, when we can easily find salt in our kitchens or at the supermarket, but salt used to be more difficult to find in many places, and it was extremely important. Salt was critical because it can be used to preserve food, and because all people need to eat at least a little salt to stay healthy. Rulers knew how important salt was, so they used it as a way of collecting money. The Chinese introduced what was likely the world's first salt tax more than 2,000 years ago, and India had salt taxes before the British arrived. But the British imposed an extremely high salt tax that collected millions of rupees from the Indian people, even though many could barely afford to pay.

The ruins of the ancestral Puebloan great house, Pueblo Bonito. The walls are more than 1,100 years old and now receive a high level of protection as part of the US National Park Service.
JOHN ELK III/GETTY IMAGES

A CAREFULLY ALIGNED MYSTERY

Pueblo Bonito is also bisected by one large wall that was carefully built in a straight line to point due north. As the sun rises above Pueblo Bonito in the morning, the wall casts a shadow on the west side, then disappears exactly at noon when it shifts to the east side. This suggests the wall was built with deep knowledge of *cosmological* purposes, but modern archaeologists still aren't sure exactly why. Another important mystery—why did the people abandon Pueblo Bonito? Ancestral Puebloans may have left in the 1300s. Many of the structures were covered by sand blowing across the desert over hundreds of years. Some archaeologists suspect there may have been a drought that lasted decades, and others speculate that the Ancestral Puebloan people cut down all the trees in the region and couldn't live without them. Whatever the reason, one thing is clear— the walls remained long after humans abandoned them.

PUEBLO BONITO WALLS

· *BUILT: 850–925* · *SOUTH WALL LENGTH: 574 feet (175 meters)*
· *WIDTH: 3 feet (0.9 meters)* · *MATERIALS: Sandstone and mud*

Indigenous Peoples built walls in North America thousands of years before Europeans arrived on the continent. A group now known as the Ancestral Puebloans built walled towns and cities across what is now the southwestern United States, where they bought and sold items like jewelry, pottery and parrots from as far away as the Gulf of Mexico. Walls gave them a relatively safe space to trade and a way to keep those goods safe. But their most impressive walled city— named Pueblo Bonito, or "beautiful town," by the Spanish—still stands as a mystery almost 1,200 years after it was built.

The Ancestral Puebloan people have been wrongly referred to as the Anasazi, or Chaco, and lived across a huge area that includes modern-day New Mexico, Colorado, Utah and Arizona. In Pueblo Bonito, they built a community that looked as much like a giant house as it did a city. It stood four or five stories high, covered 2 acres (0.8 hectares) and had almost 700 rooms! It also included 35 kivas, which were circular underground rooms containing firepits that may have been used for ceremonial purposes as well as to keep people warm. Pueblo Bonito was surrounded by large walls of brown sandstone and mud. The outer walls may have protected the people on the inside from enemies or animals. They also held the heavy timbers that supported the floors of the buildings inside.

Hadrian's Wall
c. 122–128

Antonine Wall
c. 142–154

Fossatum Africae
c. 122–128

Nine

TO SET BOUNDARIES

The Romans loved to build walls around the important cities at the heart of their empire. They also decided that barriers could serve an important purpose on the outskirts of the empire—in Britain and Africa—to mark where the Roman Empire ended and the rest of the world began.

A milecastle was a small rectangular fort built along Hadrian's Wall at regular intervals of about one Roman mile, which is a little shorter than a modern mile. Most milecastles were built with thick stone walls and had a guarded gateway that allowed people and their livestock through the wall and over a causeway that crossed the ditch on the north side of the wall. The milecastle acted as a sort of customs house, where travelers would pay taxes to the Roman Empire when coming or going. They were built near barracks houses, where 20 to 30 soldiers lived when they were not on duty.

A walking path crosses Hadrian's Wall in Northumberland, in North East England. The picturesque sycamore tree standing next to the wall won the 2016 England Tree of the Year award and has become one of the most photographed trees in Britain.
BLUE SKY IN MY POCKET/GETTY IMAGES

HADRIAN'S WALL

- *BUILT: c. 122–128* · *LENGTH: 73 miles (117 kilometers)*
- *WIDTH: Nearly 10 feet (3 meters)*
- *HEIGHT: Up to 20 feet (6 meters)* · *MATERIALS: Turf and cut stone*

When Hadrian was named Roman emperor in 117, he became ruler of a vast collection of countries and people that stretched from North Africa to northern Britain. The Romans had invaded Britain more than 70 years earlier, starting a long campaign of battles against the Celtic tribes that already lived on the island. When Hadrian became emperor, the Romans had established control over what is now southern England and Wales. But northern England and Scotland were still controlled by the Caledonians, who continued to carry out raids on the Romans' camps. Hadrian ordered the building of a wall to "separate Romans from the barbarians," as he called them.

Vallum Hadriani

The stone wall was called Vallum Hadriani in Latin, and stretched across the north of England, from the Irish Sea in the west all the way to the river Tyne, near the North Sea, in the east. Along the wall the Romans built a series of *turrets* and small forts, called milecastles, and bigger forts. Some forts were supported by as many as 1,000 soldiers, and many more people lived in nearby camps that sold the soldiers food and other things.

Three Centuries on the Line

Hadrian's Wall was an active military line for 300 years. When the Romans left Britain, many of the stones were pulled off the wall and used to build homes and other buildings. But a long stretch of the wall still stands today, next to the Hadrian's Wall Path, which is one of Britain's major tourist attractions. Some of the wall stands near the border between England and Scotland, but it has never been the border itself.

ANTONINE WALL

- **BUILT:** *c. 142–154* • **LENGTH:** *39 miles (63 kilometers)*
- **HEIGHT:** *10 feet (3 meters)* • **WIDTH:** *16 feet (5 meters)*
- **MATERIALS:** *Stone, turf and wood*

Antonius Pius became the emperor of Rome after Hadrian died. Like Hadrian, he decided the Roman Empire needed a wall along its northern border to keep Rome's enemies out and to establish exactly where that boundary lay. So 20 years after Hadrian's Wall was built, the Romans went to work on another wall. The Antonine Wall—or Vallum Antonini, as the Romans called it—was smaller and shorter than Hadrian's Wall. The new barrier stretched across Scotland, from the **Firth** of Forth to the Firth of Clyde. The wall builders laid stone foundations on the

ground, covered in **turf**, and likely placed a wooden **palisade** on top to make it more difficult to climb over. The Romans dug a deep ditch along the north side of the wall to make it even more difficult for enemies to cross the boundary. The Antonine Wall also had milecastles and Roman soldiers stationed along it. But it was abandoned after only eight years. The Romans pulled back to Hadrian's Wall to reinforce their defenses there. Some historians believe they may also have reached an agreement with the Celtic tribes that lived there to keep Scotland peaceful.

NEW TECH FOR AN ANCIENT WALL

Because Antonine Wall was made of wood and turf, there are few remains visible today, and modern scientists needed the assistance of a modern technology called *light detection and ranging,* or *LIDAR*. It's a method of collecting information by targeting an object or surface with laser light and measuring how long it takes for the reflected light to return. The measurements create 3D maps of those objects. LIDAR has been used to find fault lines that cause earthquakes in areas where lots of trees and other vegetation make it difficult to see the ground and what is under the surface. A lot of the Antonine Wall could be found easily because old historical records described where parts of it stood and because parts of the wall had been mapped as early as the 1700s. But some parts were nearly impossible to find, so LIDAR imaging was needed.

FOSSATUM AFRICAE

- **BUILT:** c. 122-128 · **LENGTH:** 466 miles (750 kilometers)
- **HEIGHT:** 9 feet (3 meters) · **WIDTH OF DITCH:** 10-20 feet (3-6 meters)
- **MATERIALS:** Stone and sand

The Romans built a lot of walls in Europe, and a few in Africa too. By winning the Third Punic War in 146 BCE, they expanded their empire into what is now Algeria and Tunisia. And to make it clear where their territory ended, they built the Fossatum Africae. The Romans built a wall of dry stones in some places, but most of the Fossatum Africae was more a ditch than an actual wall. It ran along the southern edge of the new Roman province of Africa. The ditch was not supposed to keep enemy armies out but instead make it clear where Roman Africa ended and the territory of its next-door neighbor and ally, *Numidia*, started.

From Sea to Sea
It stretched from the north coast of the promontory to the southeastern coast.

That first frontier ditch was called the Fossa Regia. Archaeologists and historians aren't sure when the rest of the Fossatum Africae was built. It likely took many years, maybe hundreds, to finish. It may have been started after Hadrian (who commissioned the wall that bears his name in northern England) visited in 122 and continued off and on for the next 200 years. The only written reference to the Fossatum Africae was in the *Codex Theodosianus*, written hundreds of years later which urged Roman citizens in Africa to maintain the Fossatum Africae or lose their land rights. The Romans eventually abandoned the Fossatum Africae after the Vandal Kingdom conquered the area in the 430s.

The darker shaded region of this map shows the approximate reach of the Roman province of Africa in 146 BCE. The Fossatum Africae was built along the southern edge of Roman occupation. Few hints of it remain today.
T8612/WIKIMEDIA COMMONS/CC BY-SA 4.0. ADAPTED FROM ORIGINAL

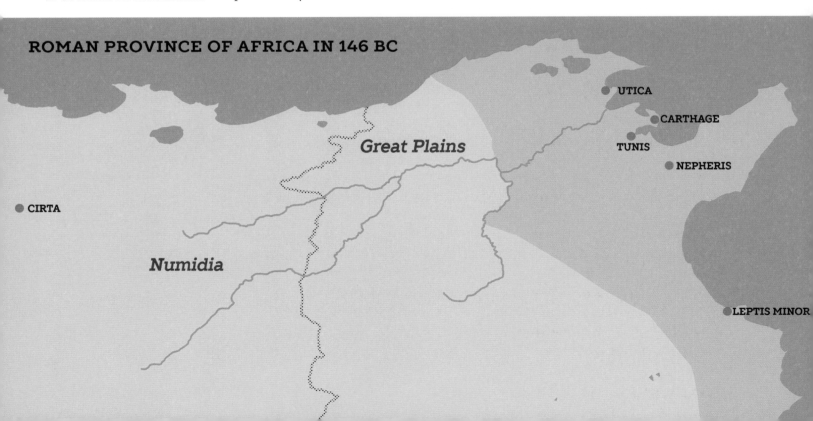

ROMAN PROVINCE OF AFRICA IN 146 BC

UTICA

CARTHAGE

TUNIS

NEPHERIS

CIRTA

Great Plains

Numidia

LEPTIS MINOR

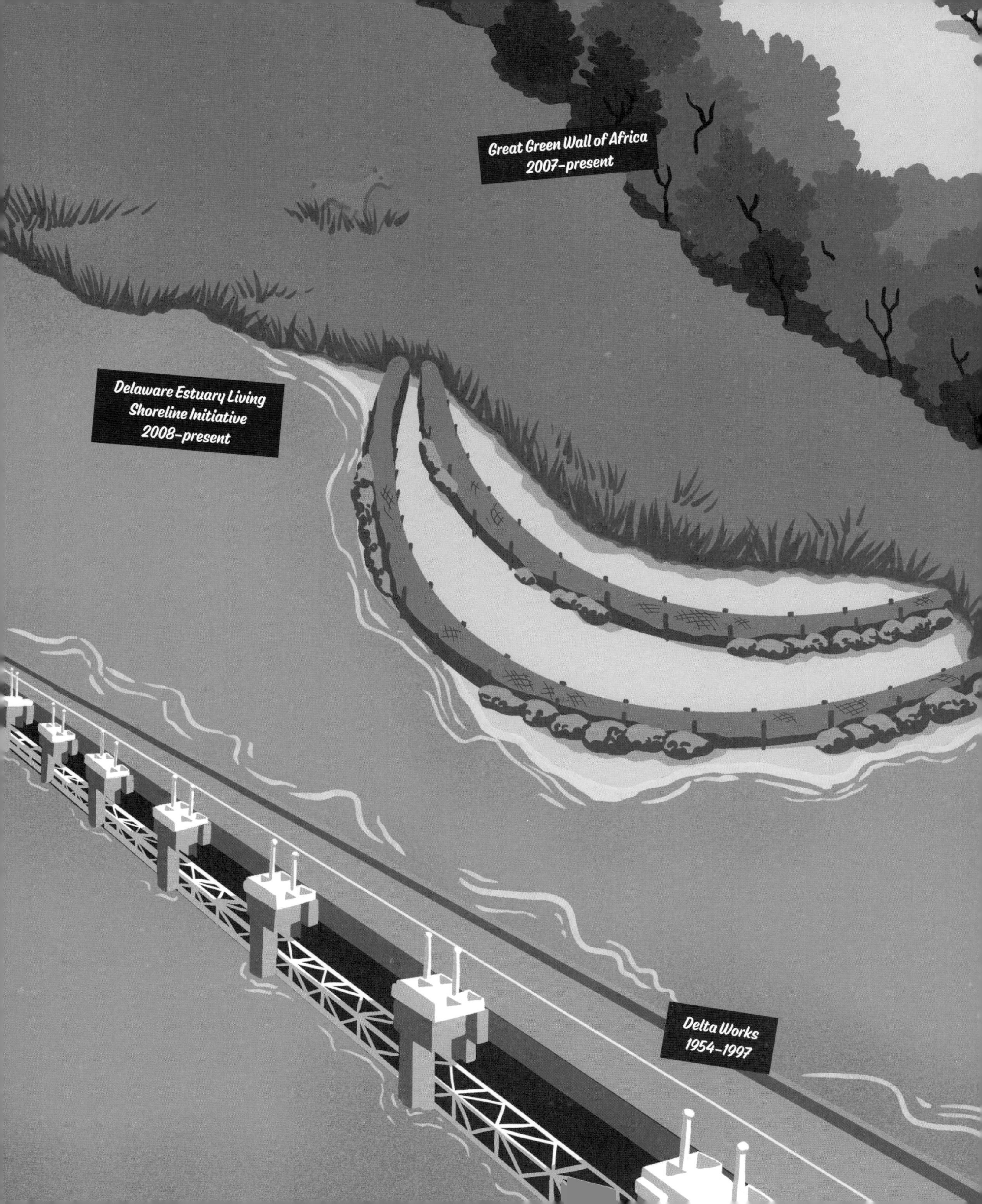

Great Green Wall of Africa
2007–present

Delaware Estuary Living
Shoreline Initiative
2008–present

Delta Works
1954–1997

Ten

TO PROTECT THE PLANET

Humans have built walls from stone and bricks for thousands of years, but barriers in the future may take other forms, and they may help protect the future of both people and the planet. These future barriers will use nature to stop the worst effects of climate change and, hopefully, help the planet and its people heal.

GREAT GREEN WALL OF CHINA

People in China have been creating a great green wall for many years. The Three-North Shelter Forest Program—as it's officially called—is a massive effort to plant a series of windbreaking forests along the edge of the Gobi Desert, in northern China. The first trees were planted in 1978, and China says it will keep planting trees in the region until 2050. It will provide some firewood for the people who live nearby, but the main reason for planting this long strip of forests is to stop the spread of the Gobi Desert and the massive windstorms that blow out of the dusty region and cover farmland as far away as South Korea and Japan. The project has had problems along the way—many trees died soon after planting, and some people complained that the surviving trees soaked up too much water, which made it difficult to farm nearby. Still, many in China have high hopes for these forests and predict that the Great Green Wall will eventually stretch 2,800 miles (4,500 kilometers).

GREAT GREEN WALL OF AFRICA

- *PLANTED: 2007–present* • *GOAL: 4,971 miles (8,000 kilometers)*
- *COUNTRIES TAKING PART: 11* • *MATERIAL: Trees*
- *TREES TO BE PLANTED: Billions*

Instead of building yet another wall, many Africans are now planting a green barrier that might grow into the next wonder of the world, and stop the process of *desertification* and spread of the Sahara Desert. It's an ambitious plan to plant a line of trees across Africa, along the edge of the desert. The Sahara is one of the driest places on earth. It's also one of the poorest.

Millions of Africans have suffered from climate change, drought, famine and poverty, but the Great Green Wall could help them fight those problems in the future. As the trees take root and forests grow, the land will be rejuvenated and better able to grow food for people to eat. That should create farming jobs for Africans. It will also store more rainwater and help local people make it through dry spells. As the trees grow, they'll also help fight climate change by absorbing carbon dioxide and releasing oxygen back into the atmosphere. The Great Green Wall is a huge project that will take years, but the United Nations predicts it could rejuvenate 247 million acres (100 million hectares) of barren land, suck 250 million tons of carbon out of the atmosphere and create 10 million jobs in sustainable agriculture and energy by 2030. Many Africans are now dreaming of what could be the world's largest living structure—three times bigger than the Great Barrier Reef.

DELAWARE ESTUARY LIVING SHORELINE INITIATIVE

- *BUILT: 2008–present*
- *SIZE OF ESTUARY: 6,800 square miles (17,600 square kilometers)*
- *SIZE OF WETLAND: 400,000 acres (1,600 square kilometers)*
- *SPECIES: More than 200*

The Delaware Estuary is the large tidal mouth of the Delaware River, where the fresh water flows out into the salty water of Delaware Bay and into the Atlantic Ocean. A lot of the estuary is covered in soggy marshland—which is flooded in winter or at high tide. Marshes are incredibly important for wildlife because they provide habitat for birds and fish. Marshes also act as giant filters, cleaning huge amounts of water. And they protect nearby towns and cities from flooding by soaking up additional water in storms and at high tide. But climate change is causing ocean levels to rise, and that means the Delaware Estuary may not be as helpful to the birds and fish and humans who live around it. Luckily, some people who live in the states of Delaware, New Jersey and Pennsylvania came up with a plan to protect the estuary by building a living wall.

A Natural Fix

The Delaware Estuary Living Shoreline Initiative—DELSI for short—doesn't call for concrete or steel. Natural products like wooden stakes and logs made out of coconut husks are used to create long reefs for mussels and other shellfish. When enough shellfish move in and take over the reef, they stabilize the edge of the marshland and prevent it from eroding into the ocean. These natural barriers have already been tested in other American states, and we will see more living shorelines in the years to come.

The world's longest human-built dyke is the Saemangeum Seawall in South Korea. It stretches 21 miles (33 kilometers) across the Saemangeum estuary and was built to create 150 square miles (400 square kilometers) of farmland and a freshwater reservoir out of low-lying land that was covered by the Yellow Sea. Environmental groups opposed the plan when it was first announced in the 1990s and challenged it in court before construction was finally allowed to go ahead. Opponents argued the mudflats already acted as natural water purifiers. They also worried it would destroy the mudflats, which provide critical habitat for wild animals. The area had been a feeding ground for as many as half a million shorebirds, including at least two endangered species. Birdwatchers say the number of shorebirds returning to the area has declined significantly since the seawall was finished in 2010. But the companies that built the seawall say the increase in food-growing land is a win for the planet, as is the construction of a large floating solar farm near the seawall that will provide South Korea with clean, renewable electricity.

DELTA WORKS
• BUILT: 1954–1997 • LENGTH: 18.5 miles (30 kilometers)
• MATERIALS: Steel and concrete

The Netherlands is one of the lowest, flattest countries in the world. The name itself means "lower countries." The average elevation of the country is 98.5 feet (30 meters), and an area called Zuidplaspolder is the lowest at 23 feet (7 meters) below sea level. So climate change and rising sea levels are huge concerns. But a long series of ocean walls, called Delta Works, protects the Netherlands from the nasty storm surges of the North Sea.

Construction started in 1954 and continued for decades because of the difficulty of building such a long structure that stands in the sea. The longest segment is a dam called the Oosterscheldekering, which stretches 5.6 miles (9 kilometers) between two islands and is a key link in the longer series of dams, storm-surge barriers, dykes, locks and levees that protect low-lying land in the country's southwest. The American Society of Civil Engineers hailed the Delta Works as one of the Seven Wonders of the Modern World.

THE LINE
An unusual construction project began in the Saudi desert in 2021 that has promised to house millions of people, use nothing but renewable energy and preserve nature. The Line is a proposed linear city that could one day be 110 miles (180 kilometers) long and no wider than 660 feet (200 meters). The plan calls for two extremely long buildings stretching side by side across the desert, with an outdoor space between them. The city would have no cars, but residents could walk to most of the things they need in five minutes or less, or take an underground train for anything farther than that. Some people have praised The Line as a good project for the environment and for Saudi Arabia's economy. Critics complain that it will force the al-Huwaitat Indigenous People to move and that it could create a barrier for birds and other wildlife that migrate across the desert every year.

WALLS OR BRIDGES?
It's been said that people build too many walls and not enough bridges. Looking back on thousands of years of human history, it's hard to argue with that. And looking into the future, it's just as hard to imagine people stopping. Walls are simply too effective at keeping people, animals and nature out. But history has also shown that walls can help—they can protect us, feed us, keep us safe. Walls can protect the planet too. Let's hope that in the years and decades ahead, people will choose to build walls that protect all and exclude no one.

GLOSSARY

barracks—buildings used to house soldiers

bedrock—solid rock under loose ground soil

berm—a raised, flat bank of land next to a river or canal

Bible—the Christian holy book, consisting of the Old and New Testaments

bureaucracy—a system of government run by state officials rather than by elected representatives

Catholics—members of the Roman Catholic Church

ceasefire—an agreement between two warring sides to stop fighting

citadel—a fortress on high ground that protects or controls a city

communist—adhering to a system of government in which all things are owned and shared by everyone

concentration camps—centers where political prisoners, refugees or members of minority groups are imprisoned and often exploited, punished and even killed

conquistador—a conqueror, especially one of the Spanish conquerors of Mexico and Peru in the 16th century

cosmological—relating to the study of the origin and development of the universe

desertification—the loss of plant life on land due to human activities and changing climate

erosion—the process by which soil and other earthen materials are worn away and transported by natural forces such as wind or water

favelas—slums or shantytowns on the outskirts of Brazil's large cities

firth—a narrow inlet of the sea, usually the lower part of an estuary (a place where river water mixes with tidal ocean water)

guerrilla war—a form of irregular warfare in which members of independent units use harassment, sabotage and other military tactics to fight a larger traditional military

immigration—the movement of people into other countries, where they become permanent residents or citizens

Indigenous—term that describes the earliest known inhabitants of a place

kilns—furnaces or ovens in which substances are burned, baked or dried

Koran—the sacred book of Islam, believed by Muslims to be the word of Allah, or God

LIDAR—a 3D scanning technology that works on the principle of radar but uses light from a laser

loess—a loosely compacted yellow-gray deposit of windblown sediment

migrants—people who move from one place to another, especially in order to find work or better living conditions

Ming dynasty—the rulers of China from 1368 to 1644

moats—water-filled ditches that surround a fort or town as a defense against attack

mortar—a flexible paste that is spread between building blocks like stones and bricks and holds them together as it hardens

nomads—people with no fixed residence who move from place to place

Numidia—an ancient kingdom in northwest Africa, made up of what is modern-day Algeria, Tunisia, Libya and parts of Morocco

optical dating—a technique for determining how long ago a mineral sediment was last exposed to sunlight; also known as optically stimulated luminescence, or OSL, dating

palisade—a strong fence made of wooden or iron stakes

parallel—one of the imaginary circles on Earth's surface that parallel the equator and mark latitude

predators—animals that naturally prey on other animals

promontory—a point of high land that juts into a large body of water

Protestants—members of any of the western Christian churches that are separate from the Roman Catholic Church and follow the principles of the reformation

radar—a system for detecting the direction and distance of objects by sending out pulses of high-frequency electromagnetic waves that are reflected back to the source

radiocarbon dating—a method of determining the age of carbon-based materials

ramparts—defensive walls of a castle or walled city, having a broad top with a walkway and typically a stone parapet

refugees—people who have been forced to leave their country in order to escape war, persecution or natural disaster

rupee—the basic monetary unit of India, Pakistan, Sri Lanka, Nepal, Mauritius and the Seychelles

siege—a military operation in which enemy forces surround a town or building, cutting off essential supplies

Silk Road—a network of trade routes connecting the East and West from the 2nd century BCE to the 15th century

smallpox—an acute contagious viral disease causing fever and pustules, usually leaving permanent scars. It had been effectively eradicated through vaccination by 1980.

smuggling—the illegal movement of goods in or out of a country

surveillance—close observation, especially of a suspected spy or criminal

taxes—compulsory payments to the government from workers' income or business profits

terraces—flat areas made in a hillside to increase the amount of land that can be cultivated

trapezoid—a four-sided shape with only one pair of parallel sides

turf—a surface layer of earth containing grass and its roots

turrets—small towers on top of a larger tower or at the corner of a building or wall on a castle

UNESCO World Heritage site—a landmark or area designated by the United Nations Educational, Scientific and Cultural Organization as having cultural, historical, scientific or some other significance

United Nations—an organization of the world's countries to maintain international peace and security

veteran—a former member of the armed forces

Vietnam War—a military conflict in Southeast Asia from 1955 to 1975 that involved North and South Vietnam and eventually Laos, Cambodia and the United States

RESOURCES

PRINT

Finch, Dawn. *Hadrian's Wall*. Raintree, 2019.

Holdgrafer, Brad. *Walls*. Princeton Architectural Press, 2018.

Lin, Jillian. *The Emperor Who Built the Great Wall*. Jillian Lin Books, 2016.

Perkins, Mitali. *Between Us and Abuela: A Family Story from the Border*. Farrar, Straus and Giroux, 2019.

ONLINE

Athens Long Walls: livius.org/articles/place/athens/athens-photos/athens-long-walls

Berlin Wall: bbc.com/news/world-europe-50013048

Brazil Favelas: weforum.org/agenda/2022/08/mit-favelas-brazil-lidar

Delaware Estuary Living Shorelines: delawareestuary.org/science-and-research/living-shorelines

Dingo Fence: smithsonianmag.com/smart-news/australias-dingo-proof-fence-changing-ecosystem-outback-180963273

Dubrovnik Walls: wallsofdubrovnik.com/history

Friendship Park, San Diego–Tijuana: friendshippark.org

Great Green Wall of Africa: thegreatgreenwall.org/about-great-green-wall

Great Wall of China: whc.unesco.org/en/list/438

Great Wall of Gorgan: whc.unesco.org/en/tentativelists/6199

Great Wall of India: atlasobscura.com/places/great-wall-india

Great Zimbabwe: education.nationalgeographic.org/resource/great-zimbabwe

Korean Demilitarized Zone: history.com/topics/korea/demilitarized-zone

Kuélap: perunorth.com/kuelap

Lugo City Walls: whc.unesco.org/en/list/987

Machu Picchu: whc.unesco.org/en/list/274

Maginot Line: history.com/topics/world-war-ii/maginot-line

Moroccan Western Sahara Wall: atlasobscura.com/places/moroccan-wall-of-western-sahara

Northern Ireland Peace Walls: cbc.ca/radio/ideas/the-peace-walls-of-belfast-do-they-still-help-keep-the-peace-1.5262640

Pueblo Bonito: sah-archipedia.org/buildings/NM-01-045-0056

Quebec City Walls: quebec-cite.com/en/old-quebec-city/inside-quebec-citys-walls

Sacsayhuamán: worldhistory.org/Sacsayhuaman

Theodosian Walls: worldhistory.org/Theodosian_Walls

Vietnam Veterans Memorial Wall: vvmf.org/about-the-wall/

Warsaw Ghetto: theholocaustexplained.org/the-camps/the-warsaw-ghetto-a-case-study

ACKNOWLEDGMENTS

Thanks first and foremost to my wife, Rebecca, who has climbed over, retreated from, thrown stones at, pounded her fists on and finally walked around more metaphorical walls with me than I can remember. I love you, Becky. Thanks also to my three sons, Lochlan, Benji and Charlie, who have always supported their dad being a writer and always shown an interest in what I'm writing. Far beyond this book, I am thankful for my mum, Betty, and thankful to her for everything she's done for me right from the start. The same can be said for my sister, Gillian, who was born two and a half years after me but has shown me on many occasions that people can learn important lessons from people who are younger than they are.

I would also like to thank my friends and colleagues at the Canadian Broadcasting Corporation. Working as a journalist for CBC Radio is a privilege, and working with the people I work with has been a blessing. Not only are they kind and funny, but they teach me something new every day. We should all be so fortunate to learn and laugh every day we go to work!

I'd like to thank everyone at Orca Book Publishers for all they do. Thank you to Kirstie Hudson for guiding me through the imagining and writing of this book, and for helping me find another home for my writing. Thank you to Ruth Linka and Andrew Wooldridge for once again being willing to publish a book that I wanted to write. And thank you to everyone and anyone at Orca who works so hard to bring so many good books to young readers—Georgia Bradburne, Rachel Page, Olivia Gutjahr, Diane McDonald, Kennedy Cullen and Sarah Howden.

Finally, thank you to all the librarians, teachers and bookstore owners who purchased my first children's book, *Why Humans Build Up*, and, of course, to all the children who read it!

INDEX   *Page numbers in **bold** indicate an image caption.*

GREGOR CRAIGIE is a radio journalist and writer. He has worked for the Canadian Broadcasting Corporation for many years. Before that he worked in several cities, including London, England, where he was an announcer for the BBC World Service and a reporter for CBS Radio. Gregor's first book for adults, *On Borrowed Time: North America's Next Big Quake*, was a finalist for the Writers' Trust Balsillie Prize for Public Policy and the City of Victoria Butler Book Prize. His first book for children was *Why Humans Build Up: The Rise of Temples, Towers and Skyscrapers*, part of the Orca Timeline series. He lives in Victoria, British Columbia.

ARDEN TAYLOR is a Toronto-based freelance illustrator. A graduate of Sheridan College with an honors bachelor of illustration, she enjoys digitally creating colorful illustrations of architecture and people and designs for wallpaper and other projects. Her clients include *Hazlitt Magazine* and the California Institute of Technology, and her work has been featured in various magazines, newspapers, advertising campaigns and websites.